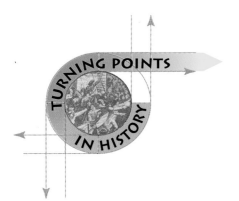

The Fall of the Bastille

Revolution in France

STEWART ROSS

Heinemann
LIBRARY

H www.heinemann.co.uk
Visit our website to find out more information about Heinemann Library books.

To order:
☎ Phone 44 (0) 1865 888066
▤ Send a fax to 44 (0) 1865 314091
▭ Visit the Heinemann Bookshop at www.heinemann.co.uk to browse our catalogue and order online.

First published in Great Britain by Heinemann Library, Halley Court, Jordan Hill, Oxford OX2 8EJ, a division of Reed Educational and Professional Publishing Ltd. Heinemann is a registered trademark of Reed Educational & Professional Publishing Limited.

OXFORD MELBOURNE AUCKLAND JOHANNESBURG BLANTYRE
GABORONE IBADAN PORTSMOUTH NH (USA) CHICAGO

Produced for Heinemann Library by Discovery Books Limited
Designed by Ian Winton
Illustrations by Stefan Chabluk
Printed in Hong Kong

05 04 03 02 01
10 9 8 7 6 5 4 3 2 1

ISBN 0 431 06905 0

British Library Cataloguing in Publication Data

Ross, Stewart, 1947–
The fall of the Bastille : revolution in France. - (Turning points in history)
1. France - History - Storming of the Bastille, 1789 - Juvenile literature
2. France - History - Revolution, 1789-1799 - Juvenile literature
I. Title
944'.041

Acknowledgements
The Publishers would like to thank the following for permission to reproduce photographs:
The Art Archive, pp. 5, 12, 14, 21; *Mary Evans*, pp. 4, 7, 9, 10, 11, 13, 15, 26; *Hulton-Deutsch Collection*, pp. 16, 17, 22; *Hulton Getty*, pp. 18, 19, 23; *Peter Newark's Historical Pictures*, pp. 6, 8, 24, 25, 28; *Peter Newark's Military Pictures*, p. 29.

Cover photographs reproduced with the permission of The Art Archive

Every effort has been made to contact copyright holders of any material reproduced in this book. Any omissions will be rectified in subsequent printings if notice is given to the Publisher.

Any words appearing in the text in bold, **like this**, are explained in the Glossary.

Contents

Revolution!

Siege

Bernard-René de Launay, commander of the Bastille, was frightened. He had only 114 men to defend his ancient fortress-prison and its enormous cache of gunpowder. Beyond the walls milled a bloodthirsty mob of over a thousand Parisians. Determined to force their way in, they had trained their cannon on the Bastille's raised wooden drawbridge.

Surrender

De Launay considered his options. He could blow up the Bastille, fight it out, or surrender. At about 5 pm, he made up his mind. The soldiers inside the Bastille stopped firing and, as a white handkerchief fluttered on one of its high towers, a note was shoved through a gap in the drawbridge boards.

The besiegers pushed a plank across the moat. Balancing across the makeshift bridge, a young man grabbed the note and read it. The Bastille would surrender! Minutes later, the mob was surging forward to take its prize.

Victory! A guard of the Bastille passes out a note from Governor de Launay saying that the fortress will surrender.

Triumph of the people

The Bastille fell on Tuesday 14 July 1789. Although it was not the beginning of the French Revolution, it was an important turning point. The Bastille was a symbol of royal power and **tyranny**. Its capture marked the

victory of ordinary people over King Louis XVI. More alarming, the mob's victory set the violent tone of the years to come.

The French Revolution changed France for ever. It also had a huge impact on both Europe and elsewhere. As a result, the fall of the Bastille is now seen as one of the most significant events in modern history.

A romantic impression of the storming of the Bastille. The walls of the fortress are shown much taller than they really were to exaggerate the achievement of the attackers.

WHAT IS A REVOLUTION?

A revolution is a rapid, total and permanent change. Historians use the term in several different ways. The French Revolution was basically a political revolution, although social and economic changes followed from it. Other types of revolution include the much slower Industrial Revolution that began in the late 18th century, and saw the introduction of machines to do work that had once been done by hand. It was the most important economic change to affect human society since the beginning of farming and as a result trade, industry and population all grew at a tremendous rate. More recently, the modern Communications Revolution, has brought us computers, the Internet and mobile phones, completely changing the way we work and live.

The Ancien Regime

Three estates

France's government and society before the Revolution is known as the '**Ancien Regime**'. It was headed by the king. Everyone else belonged to one of three '**estates**': the **Nobility**, the Church and the Third Estate (ordinary people, the great majority of the population). Wealthy, middle-class members of the Third Estate were known as the '**bourgeoisie**'.

Between them, the king, nobility and church owned most of the land. The nobles and the church enjoyed many ancient privileges, such as not paying personal taxes. The nobles held many of the best jobs, especially in the army and the church. Because the whole inflexible system was based upon **inherited privilege**, it benefited the few at the expense of the many.

Louis XVI in his coronation robes. Although he inherited great power he proved to be an incompetent king.

The causes of the Revolution

The Ancien Regime did not suddenly collapse. Difficulties had been building up for years, and the fall of the Bastille came after a long chain of crises.

Historians have debated endlessly about the causes of the French Revolution. Some say it was a class struggle between the privileged groups, the bourgeoisie and ordinary people. Others stress the importance of revolutionary ideas. Another point of view is that the Ancien Regime could have reformed itself but was brought down by incompetent management.

The king and queue

Because the king was responsible for running the government, he must take quite a lot of responsibility for what happened. King Louis XVI was well-meaning but lacked the intelligence, judgement and strength of character needed for his difficult job. Louis was not helped by his marriage in 1770 to the Austrian princess Marie Antoinette. Instead of helping him, she annoyed both **courtiers** and ordinary people with her tactless comments and behaviour. For example, she opposed ministers' attempts to sort out France's finances.

The royal palace of Versailles. Louis XIV built the palace outside Paris, at the end of the 17th century, to separate himself and his court from the troublesome Paris mob.

ROYAL WEAKNESS

A year before the fall of the Bastille, the king's sister, Madam Elizabeth, remarked how her brother seemed incapable of making a firm decision and sticking to it, saying: *'The king is back-tracking. He is always afraid of making mistakes. Once he has made a decision, he is terrified that he might have got it wrong. I believe that in government, as in education, one should not say "Let it be done" until one is sure of being right.'*

The burden of debt

Bankruptcy

In the end, Louis XVI's government collapsed because it was **bankrupt**. This was not because France itself was poor – it was the wealthiest country in continental Europe. The problem was that for many years the government spent more than it earned. To make up the difference, it borrowed. When Louis XVI came to the throne in 1774 he **inherited** a debt of 4 billion **livres**.

The government paid **interest** on the money it borrowed. To pay this interest, it borrowed more. Therefore it had to pay more interest ... so the vicious circle continued. In 1789 the government was spending 300 million livres (more than half its income) in interest. This debt was made worse by France's involvement in the American War of Independence (1775-83).

Reform

There were two ways out of the government's difficulty: either cutting back on spending or increasing income. Under Louis' feeble leadership it managed neither.

Peasants paying their taxes. One of the most unfair things about the Ancien Regime was that the rich nobles did not have to pay some of the heaviest taxes.

Most government income came from taxation. There were two types of tax. Indirect taxes, such as **customs duty** and the *gabelle* (salt tax), were paid by everyone. There were also direct taxes on personal wealth paid by the peasants and **bourgeoisie** but not by the **privileged nobles** or officials. Many people thought this grossly unfair, especially as most nobles were very well off and the majority of peasants lived in poverty.

Anne-Robert Turgot, Louis XVI's first finance minister, tried to reform the system. His ideas met with howls of complaint from the privileged classes and he resigned. His successor went on borrowing.

In 1787, finance minister Charles de Calonne found no one would lend the government any more money. As a last resort, he called a meeting of all the country's privileged groups (the Assembly of Notables) and asked them to help. When they refused it became clear that the **Ancien Regime** was running out of time.

Mᴿ NECKER.

Jacques Necker (1732–1804) who succeeded Charles de Calonne as finance minister was also unable to do anything about the country's bankruptcy, but he became a popular hero when he asked the king to summon the Estates General.

Representatives of the people

The nearest thing France had to a parliament was the Estates General. This gathering of the three **estates** had not met since 1614. In its absence, thirteen supreme law courts (known as **Parlements**) claimed they represented the people of France. The most important was the Parlement of Paris. In fact, the Parlements represented only the church and privileged landowners. This particularly irritated the wealthy bourgeoisie who dominated the Third Estate. They deeply resented their lack of political influence in the governing of France.

Crisis

No way out

With no money, Louis XVI and his government were powerless. The king, while still popular with the masses, had lost the respect of his court. The queen became mixed up in scandal and was very unpopular. The **privileged** classes had refused to help. The **bourgeoisie** did not believe the king wanted reform. And every day the government's debt got bigger.

The Estates General

The Paris **Parlement** managed to persuade people that it could save the country. Not knowing what to do, Louis banished it from the capital in August 1787, recalled it the next month, dismissed it again and, in May 1788, recalled it again.

The Parlement, however, had nothing new to offer. In August 1788 the king bowed to popular pressure and agreed to summon the Estates General the following May. It would be the first time for over 150 years that representatives of the three **estates** of the realm had met.

The Third Estate

The king's decision to summon the Estates General sparked a new row. Should the three estates (**Nobility**, Church and Third Estate) meet together or separately? And should the Third Estate have the same number of representatives as each of the other two estates, or a number equal to both of them combined?

Queen Marie Antoinette. She was famously out of touch with the lives of ordinary people. A story spread among the poor that when the Queen heard they had no bread, she replied, 'Let them eat cake!' This rumour infuriated the hungry people of Paris and in October 1789 thousands of women set off for Versailles chanting, 'Cut the queen's head off!'

Again Louis gave way to popular pressure. Although he overruled the Parlement and agreed that the estates should meet separately, he did accept double representation for the Third Estate. Of the 610 **deputies** elected to the Third Estate most belonged to the bourgeoisie and represented the views of professionals like lawyers, industrialists, merchants and bankers. Only a handful were peasants.

Meanwhile, the mood in the country was ugly. Bad harvests had forced up the price of bread. Faced with starvation, the poor of Paris and other cities were on the verge of revolt.

THE PRICE OF BREAD

The main food of most French families was the four-pound loaf of bread. It normally cost eight **sous**. By February 1789 its price in Paris had almost doubled to fifteen sous – more than half the average daily wage of a typical worker. A family of four needed two loaves a day, which many could not afford. Small wonder a worker asked of representatives of the Third Estate, *'Are they concerned with us? Are they thinking of lowering the price of bread? We haven't eaten anything for two days.'*

The beginning of revolution? The three estates (nobles, clergy and common people) go in procession to Versailles for the opening of the Estates General.

Enlightenment

New thinking

Over the previous 75 years, **radical** new ideas had spread across Europe. In France, they changed the way many people regarded the **Ancien Regime**. As a result some people came to believe that even a reformed Ancien Regime was not enough – they wanted a different system altogether.

Reason, rights and contracts

Historians call the new thinking the 'Enlightenment'. It held that reason, rather than faith or tradition, was the best guide to how things should be done. Enlightened thinkers like the Frenchman François de Voltaire (1694–1778) shocked many people by arguing that most religion was just superstition. His followers wanted to abolish the church's wealth and **privileges**.

Voltaire, whose ideas helped undermine the Ancien Regime. As a young man he was imprisoned in the Bastille for attacking the government.

Some enlightened thinkers spoke of 'natural rights' – the privileges that every human being had, which could not be taken away. They included such things as the right not to be imprisoned without a fair trial. Supporters of the Enlightenment also admired the British system of parliamentary democracy. They agreed with the English thinker John Locke (1632–1704) who said government should be based on a contract between the governors and the people they governed. If the governors broke this contract by not governing well, the people had a right to change them. French thinkers like Charles de Montesquieu (1689–1755) and Jean-Jacques Rousseau (1712–1778) spread these ideas in France.

America's example

In 1775 Britain's colonies in America rebelled against George III because they believed his government had broken its contract with them. The American colonists believed that if you paid taxes to a monarch you were entitled to have representation within that monarch's government. The levying of unpopular taxes in the American colonies, without representation in the British Parliament, was one of the triggers of the American Revolution. The rebellion was successful and the Americans set up a new nation, the United States of America. Its **republican** system of government was based on the ideas of the Enlightenment.

France fought with America against Britain, and American ideas became all the rage in France. If Americans could have a revolution against an unfair and unpopular government, people started asking, why couldn't the French?

THE DECLARATION OF INDEPENDENCE

The Americans set out a famous expression of peoples' rights in their Declaration of Independence (1776). Its principles were not at all those of the Ancien Regime:

'We hold these truths to be self-evident, that all men are created equal, that they are endowed by their Creator with certain unalienable [unbreakable] *rights, that among these are life, liberty and the pursuit of happiness.'*

American leaders sign the Declaration of Independence in 1776. The actions of the Americans inspired the critics of the Ancien Regime in France.

The Third Estate

What is the Third Estate?

Before the Estates General met, the king asked people for their opinions and complaints. This resulted in an avalanche of papers and pamphlets offering every kind of opinion. Most took the so-called '**Patriot**' position, calling for an end to **privilege** of the wealthy few. The most influential publication came from the priest Abbé Sieyès and was called *What is the Third Estate?*

A National Assembly

In May 1789 the Estates General met at Versailles, the magnificent royal palace south of Paris. Straight away, the **deputies** chosen by the **nobles** and clergy voted to assemble in separate chambers. But the deputies elected to represent the Third Estate wanted everyone to meet together. The other **estates** wouldn't agree. So, on 17 June, the Third Estate declared it was a National Assembly representing the whole of France. It was joined by 150 clergy.

The romance of revolution. This fanciful painting by Jacques Louis David shows the Third Estate swearing the famous 'tennis court' oath.

Louis XVI now put his foot down and ordered the hall set aside for the Third Estate to be closed. Nothing daunted, on 21 June the deputies gathered in a nearby tennis court. Here they swore not to break up until France had a new, written **constitution**.

Too little, too late

Louis backed down. Two days later he told all the estates that he would bring in reforms. But he still insisted that the three estates were to remain separate. It was too little, too late. When a royal official told the Third Estate (or National Assembly) to go to their own hall, their president sent him packing with the famous words, *'the assembled nation cannot receive orders'*. It was a direct challenge to royal authority.

Louis XVI backed down yet again and told the nobles to join the National Assembly. Secretly, though, he did not approve of what had happened. While the deputies carried on talking, he ordered 20,000 troops to gather around Paris.

THE POWER OF THE PEN

Before the Estates General met, the forward-thinking priest Abbé Sieyès explained that the Third Estate represented the whole of France. This paved the way for the estate to turn itself into the National Assembly.

'The Third Estate consists of everything that belongs to the nation. And everything outside the Third Estate cannot be seen as part of the nation. So what is the Third Estate?
It is the whole of France.'

From *What is the Third Estate?*

Emanuel Sieyès was one of the few leaders to take part in almost every stage of the revolution. By 1799 he had lost his faith in democracy and helped Napoleon come to power.

To arms!

Royal power

The king said the troops were in the Paris region to keep order and protect the National Assembly. The **deputies** did not believe him. When they asked Louis to remove the troops, he refused.

Most French people backed the Assembly, but actual power remained with the king and his soldiers. So, unless something unusual happened, any hope of revolution was doomed. However, in the second week of July 1789, something unusual did happen.

Simmering violence

The common people of Paris had followed the events at Versailles with great interest. Starving and suspicious of the king and the **nobles**, they saw the National Assembly as their only hope of salvation. They believed (correctly) that the troops were gathering to crush the **Patriot** cause. Over the last few months there had been many outbreaks of violence as hungry mobs attacked grain stores, bakers and millers. On 11 July, the king dismissed Jacques Necker, the popular finance minister. When the news reached Paris the next day, the city suddenly erupted.

Mob rule. A revolutionary shoots the royal servant Jacques de Flesselles for misleading the people about where arms were kept.

People power

Stirred up by street corner **orators** like Camille Desmoulins, the Paris mob went on the rampage. When the army tried to restore order, soldiers loyal to the people sent it packing. Furious citizens, armed with stolen weapons, tore down government customs posts. A starving crowd attacked the monastery of Saint-Lazare – also a food store – and looted grain, wine and cheese.

A royal counter-attack was expected at any moment. To beat it off, the people needed weapons. They seized cannon and more than 30,000 rifles from the **Hôtel des Invalides** garrison. But they still had no gunpowder. However 250 barrels of it were stored in the Bastille, an ancient fortress used as a prison. On the morning of 14 July the mob set off to get it.

I WOULD RATHER DIE!

Camille Desmoulins, in a speech in the garden of the Palais Royal on 14 July, urged Parisians to take up arms to defend themselves.

*'Now they have forced out Necker, the **privileged** classes will do anything! Maybe tonight they are plotting to massacre the Patriots? To arms! Yes, I summon my brothers to freedom: I would rather die than submit to **servitude**!'*

Camille Desmoulins, whose speeches and writings urged the people of Paris to revolt in 1789. He was executed by the revolutionary government in 1794.

The Bastille

By command of the king

Built as a fortress in the late 14th century, the Bastille had been used as a prison for the previous 150 years. Most of its prisoners had been detained by command of the king. Some were traitors, others **heretics**, public nuisances or writers of 'dangerous' material.

An 18th century print of the Bastille showing it as it really was – an old, run-down fortress.

Some of these writers had built up the reputation of the Bastille as a grim place of rat-infested dungeons and dripping torture chambers. In fact, although there were cold and draughty rooms, prisoners who could afford to pay lived quite comfortably, with fires, curtains and furniture. They were also allowed to bring in their own possessions, food and drink.

A symbol of tyranny

By 1789 the Bastille had outlived its purpose. It was expensive to maintain and rarely held more than a handful of prisoners. In 1789 there were only seven of them.

Whatever the truth about the Bastille, however, it was still a hated symbol. Towering over the city, it represented the king's absolute power over his people. In the popular imagination it stood for repression, **privilege** and **censorship**. So when the cry went up on the morning of 14 July – *'A bas la Bastille'* ('Down with the Bastille!') – the mob responded with a fiery passion.

Two days' supplies

The Bastille's commander, Bernard-René de Launay, was in charge of his garrison of 82 retired soldiers aided by 32 Swiss guards. He also had 30 cannon, some positioned along the walls, others in the inner courtyard facing the gate.

Nevertheless, de Launay was not prepared for a siege. The Bastille had no fresh water supply and it had only enough food for two days. The mob would probably not be able to force their way in, but if relief did not come quickly he would be forced to surrender.

The man with an impossible job: Bernard-René de Launay, governor of the Bastille.

LE MARQUIS DE LAUNAY
Gouverneur de la Bastille

Né et mort à Paris, dernier gouverneur de la Bastille, entré en fonctions en 1774; à l'attaque de la forteresse, hésita entre le Roi et le peuple et résista, comptant sur des secours promis. Le peuple, mécontent, l'entraîna à l'hôtel de ville où il fut massacré sur les marches; sa tête fut promenée au bout d'une pique, pendant deux jours, dans les rues de Paris.

A nous la Bastille!

The attack begins

A mob of almost 1000 people arrived before the Bastille. Among them were a few **bourgeoisie** and a handful of soldiers who had changed sides. Most were ordinary citizens, a few of whom thought the Bastille was being used as a food store.

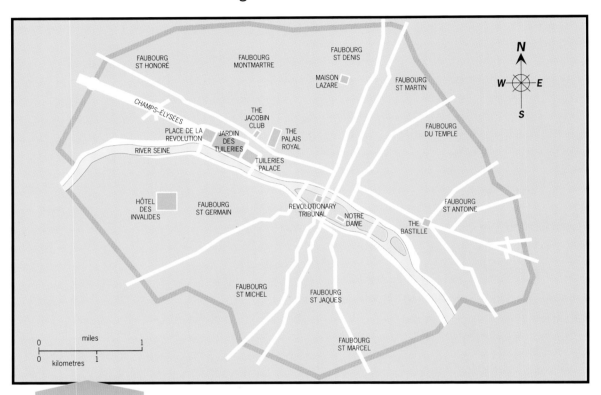

Paris at the time of the Revolution.

To begin with, representatives of the mob tried negotiating with de Launay. When nothing came of these talks, the crowd grew restless. Amid shouts of *'A nous la Bastille!'* ('Give us the Bastille!'), a number of them forced their way through the outer courtyards towards the main drawbridge.

Cannon

In mid-afternoon more soldiers arrived in support of the mob. Among them were **veterans** of the American war who took charge of operations and lined up a couple of cannon to fire at the drawbridge.

Realizing that all was probably lost, de Launay considered letting off the gunpowder in his charge. Had he done so, the explosion would have blown up the Bastille and many of the surrounding streets. In the end, though, he decided against it and surrendered.

The Bastille under siege. It is interesting to compare this view of the fortress, done after it had been captured, with the more realistic one on page 18.

De Launay's fate

As soon as the mob got inside the Bastille, they seized the gunpowder and freed the prisoners. Although ninety-eight attackers died as a result of the fight, the garrison's soldiers escaped lightly, with only a handful killed. It was de Launay who felt the full force of the people's anger.

He was dragged through the streets towards the city centre. The screaming mob kicked and spat at him as he passed. Finally, unable to take any more, he asked to die. Immediately, he was stabbed with knives, swords and bayonets. His body was kicked into the gutter and shot. Like the prisoners he held in the Bastille, he had been found guilty and punished without a trial.

A FIGHT FOR ALL THE FAMILY

The fall of the Bastille was soon exaggerated into an heroic feat of arms by the citizens of Paris. The first edition of the newspaper *Révolutions de Paris*, published on 17 July 1789, described the attack on the Bastille as a sort of family day out, attended by wives, children and grandparents:

'Women worked hard to support us, so did children. After every volley fired at us, the children ran around picking up the bullets and cannon balls. They then dodged back under cover and handed over what they had collected to our soldiers to fire back at the fortress.'

The Revolution saved

'It is a revolution'

On the evening of 14 July, the Duc de Rochefoucauld-Liancourt told the king about the fall of the Bastille. *'Is it a revolt?'* Louis asked. *'No, sire,'* the duke is supposed to have replied, *'it is a revolution'.*

This was probably the first time Louis realized how serious the situation was. His army was crumbling, his government powerless. Once the mightiest king in Europe, he now appeared to have little more power than an ordinary citizen.

The king and the Assembly

The next morning Louis visited the Assembly at Versailles. There were no trumpets, guards or **courtiers**. He came on foot and told the **deputies** that he had ordered his troops to leave Paris. The Assembly was safe.

The Marquis de Lafayette, a **veteran** of the American war, led a joyful procession that carried the news to Paris. The city's royal government was replaced with a **Patriot** one and Lafayette was put in charge of a new **militia**.

Although crowds hailed the king as a supporter of the revolution, members of the royal family knew better. On the night of 16 July one of the king's brothers and a group of his **noble** friends fled Versailles for the frontier.

The Marquis de Lafayette, one of many French soldiers who had picked up revolutionary ideas while fighting in the American Revolution, 1775-1783.

King of a free people

On 17 July – only three days after the fall of the Bastille – Louis travelled to Paris accompanied by crowds of cheering citizens. Wearing simple clothes and riding in a plain coach, he made a triumphal entry into his capital. There he read a banner announcing his new title: *'Louis XVI, Father of the French, the King of a Free People'*.

After publicly accepting the changes that had taken place, Louis appeared on a balcony before a delighted crowd. He was now just a forlorn figurehead. Real power lay with the people of Paris, and it was their colours – red and white – that Louis wore in a rosette pinned to his hat.

Louis XVI, now 'King of a Free People', arrives in Paris dressed as an ordinary citizen.

THE DECLARATION OF THE RIGHTS OF MAN

On 26 August 1789 the National Assembly issued a Declaration of the Rights of Man that set out the principles of the new France. Two of its main articles were:

Article 1. *'Men are born and remain free and equal in rights. Social distinctions may be based only upon the general good.'*

Article 3. *'Sovereignty* [political power] *rests in the nation. No body or individual may exercise any authority which does not come directly from the nation.'*

On from the Bastille

Out of control

The events of 12–14 July 1789 marked a major turning point in the revolution. First, they showed how little power the king and his government actually had. Second, they united the **bourgeoisie** and the common people. Third, they gave the more extreme revolutionaries their first taste of blood.

After the fall of the Bastille and the king's visit to Paris, there was no turning back. But once the **Ancien Regime** had been abolished, there was disagreement over what to replace it with.

The Irish politician Edmund Burke (1729–97). His best-selling book *Reflections on the Revolution in France* (1790) was read all over Europe. It encouraged European rulers to resist the French Revolution.

Replacing the Ancien Regime

To begin with France was guided by moderate reformers like Lafayette and Honore Mirabeau. They abolished the **nobles' privilege**s and titles, set up a new legal system, took over the church's land, and reorganized the country into 83 departments.

The Assembly also gave France a new **constitution**, which came into force in 1791. A Legislative Assembly replaced the old National Assembly. The king could still refuse to allow the making of laws he did not approve of. Many officials, including priests and bishops, were elected. All fairly well-off men (but no women) had a vote. So far, the revolution was just what the bourgeoisie had wanted.

The flight to Varennes

In his heart, though, Louis XVI never accepted the revolution. On 21 June 1791, he and the royal family fled from Paris and made their way in disguise towards what is now known as Belgium. They were recognized at Varennes, near the border, and brought back to Paris. As Louis had left behind a letter saying what he really thought of the revolution, from then on many saw him as a traitor.

Republic and Terror

The events in France horrified the monarchs of Europe who were afraid that their own people might rise in revolt. In April 1792 Austria and Prussia declared war on France and invaded. The Prussian commander, the Duke of Brunswick, promised to restore the Ancien Regime. The king hampered the French war effort but the Assembly refused to condemn him. Fearing that the invasion would lead to the end of the revolution, on 10 August, the people of Paris stormed the Tuileries royal palace and forced the Assembly to make France a **republic**.

Rough justice. The fate of those accused of being anti-revolutionary was settled not in the law courts but by revolutionary committees like this one.

The end of the Revolution

The death of the king

The revolution was getting more extreme and more violent. A **Convention** made up mainly of the middle-classes, replaced the Assembly in September 1792. In January 1793 it found Louis XVI guilty of treason and he was beheaded by **guillotine**. This started a 'Reign of Terror' which lasted to July 1794. During the Terror thousands of 'enemies of the people' – **nobles**, priests, wealthy **bourgeoisie** and others – were killed. Many more fled abroad to escape the violence.

'Behold the head of a traitor!' – the execution of Louis XVI. In case of trouble, the guillotine is surrounded by soldiers.

Jacobins and Girondists

Instead of concentrating on sorting out the new **republic** the Convention soon became the scene of a bitter power struggle between different bourgeoisie groups.

The radical Jacobin party, led by Maximilien Robespierre, wanted France strictly governed to preserve the Revolution. It was they who had called for the King's execution. Their opponents were the more moderate Girondists. Once the Jacobins gained control of the Convention, and the Convention's Committee of Public Safety that governed the country, they were able to use the Terror to get rid of their opponents in the Girondin party.

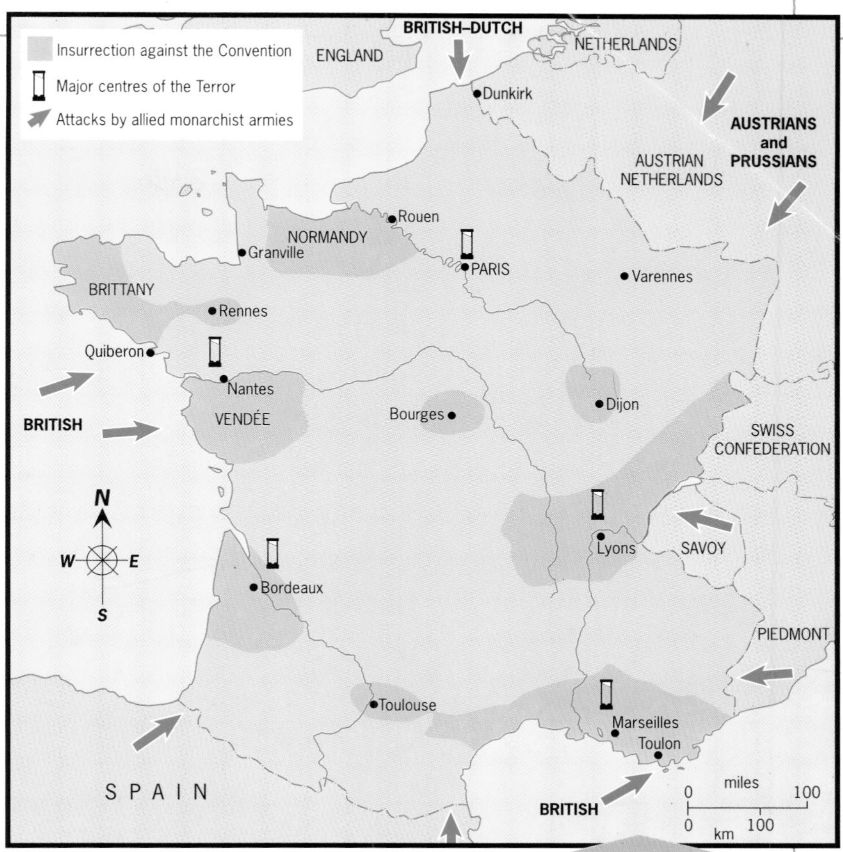

Between March 1793 and April 1794 those who went to the guillotine were not only aristocrats and priests, but bourgeoisie and peasants too. It seemed the Revolution was making victims of its own supporters.

The slaughter spread to other parts of France. In Nantes, for example, thousands of opponents of the revolution were drowned in the river Loire. Following this 100,000 more were killed in the war that broke out between Royalist and **Republican** supporters and soldiers within the region of the Vendée, in the north-west of the country.

Revolutionary France 1789–1794.

Map legend:
- Insurrection against the Convention
- Major centres of the Terror
- Attacks by allied monarchist armies

Map labels: BRITISH–DUTCH, ENGLAND, NETHERLANDS, Dunkirk, AUSTRIANS and PRUSSIANS, AUSTRIAN NETHERLANDS, Rouen, NORMANDY, Granville, PARIS, Varennes, BRITTANY, Rennes, Quiberon, Nantes, VENDÉE, Bourges, Dijon, SWISS CONFEDERATION, Lyons, SAVOY, Bordeaux, PIEDMONT, Toulouse, Marseilles, Toulon, SPAIN, BRITISH, BRITISH

The Directory

Meanwhile France found itself at war with almost every major European nation. Remarkably, the revolutionary armies beat off the invaders and advanced beyond the frontiers of France.

In July 1794 the Convention turned against Robespierre and his followers. They were removed from power and executed. The next year, a more moderate five-man council (the Directory) took over the government. It lasted until 1799, when it was overthrown by France's most successful general, Napoleon Bonaparte. Napoleon's subsequent conquests spread France's revolutionary ideals across Europe.

THE REVOLUTIONARY CALENDAR

The French revolutionaries believed they were re-making the world. They instituted the metric system for weights, measures and monetary units. They even changed the calendar. The new one had twelve months of thirty days each.

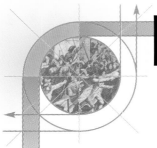

Bastille Day

Why important?

The fall of the Bastille on 14 July 1789 is the most famous event of the entire French Revolution. A vast mythology soon grew up around the event. The fortress was pictured as an enormous castle in which hundreds of miserable wretches were chained in damp and dingy dungeons. Its capture was told as a bloody battle marked by deeds of incredible courage.

But as we have seen, the old fortress was an unimportant prison that surrendered easily after unheroic fighting. So what made the fall of the Bastille so famous?

The New France

The importance of the fall of the Bastille was largely symbolic. The building mattered because it had housed critics of the **Ancien Regime** detained without trial by *lettres de cachet*. Its fall showed the power of ordinary people – soldiers, shopkeepers, housewives, servants – acting together.

The French Revolution and the rule of Napoleon changed France forever. Although the monarchy was restored for a time, it was replaced for good by a **republic** in 1848. The **nobles'** power and **privilege** were much reduced. The Roman Catholic church also lost much of its wealth and influence. The new France was based upon the rule of law and the right to

A poster of 1793 urging citizens to defend their new republic to the death. The revolutionary call to arms still stirs French hearts in the words of their national anthem, the *Marseillaise*.

UNITÉ
INDIVISIBILITÉ
DE LA
RÉPUBLIQUE
LIBERTÉ
ÉGALITÉ
FRATERNITÉ
OU LA
MORT

speak freely and enjoy one's own property. These changes greatly helped the **bourgeoisie**, who became France's new ruling class. Only gradually did the benefits of the new regime filter down to the workers and peasant farmers.

Wider Significance

French armies spread the principles of the Enlightenment and the Revolution over much of Europe. This made the fall of the Bastille significant for the whole continent. It marked the beginning of the end of the old Europe, controlled by all-powerful kings and emperors. In its place the modern, democratic Europe of today began gradually to emerge.

BASTILLE DAY

The Bastille story inspired the attack on the royal palace in 1792, and further French revolutions in 1830 and 1848. Not surprisingly, when in 1880 France established a National Day, it chose the anniversary of the fall of the Bastille – 14 July. Bastille Day is still an annual holiday. It begins the traditional summer vacation season and is marked by parades, parties, speeches and firework displays. As well as shouting *'Vive le 14 juillet!'* ('Long live the 14th of July!'), crowds also use the slogan first heard over 200 years ago: *'A bas la Bastille!'*

A modern Bastille Day military parade in Paris.

Time-line

1762	Rousseau's book *The Social Contract* is published	
1774	Louis XVI becomes king	
1775–83	American War of Independence	
1786	Charles de Calonne presents his reforms to Louis XVI	
1787	Assembly of Notables meets	
1789	5 May	Estates General meets
	17 June	Third Estate becomes the National Assembly
	20 June	National Assembly swears the 'tennis court' oath
	14 July	Fall of the Bastille
	26 August	National Assembly agrees the Declaration of the Rights of Man
1790	France is organized into 83 departments. Law is reorganized. Parlements are abolished.	
1791	Royal family flees from Paris and is recaptured at Varennes. Legislative Assembly meets.	
1792	War with Austria and Prussia. France is declared a republic. Lafayette flees the country. French forces occupy the lands now known as Belgium.	
1793	Louis XVI is executed. Committee of Public Safety set up in March to help run the country. War with Britain, Holland and Spain. 'Reign of Terror' begins (ends in 1794).	
1794	Robespierre is executed	
1795	Louis XVII, son of Louis XVI, dies in prison. Directory is set up.	
1796–7	Napoleon conquers Italy	
1804	Napoleon crowned emperor	
1815	France restores the monarchy. Louis XVIII becomes king.	
1848	France becomes a republic again	
1880	Bastille Day (14 July) becomes France's National Day	

Glossary

Ancien Regime	French society and government before the revolution, based on a rigid class and privilege system
bankrupt	with no money to pay debts
bourgeoisie	wealthy middle-class people
censorship	the suppression of certain facts in writing or other media
constitution	the laws and customs by which a country is governed
Convention	a sort of parliament called without the king's permission
courtier	someone who attends the royal court
customs duty	taxes paid on goods entering and leaving a country
deputy	someone chosen to represent the views of others
estate	one of the three groups (nobles, priests and the common people) that made up society in the Ancien Regime
guillotine	a beheading machine
heretic	someone who disagrees with the church's teaching
Hôtel des Invalides	a military hospital in Paris that was sometimes used as a garrison
inherited	anything that is passed on from parent to child
interest	the charge a borrower pays someone who lends them money
literate	able to read and write
livre	the main French unit of currency in the Ancien Regime. In the 1790s a new decimal currency based on the franc was established. A new franc was worth slightly more than the old livre.
militia	a defence force
nobility, nobles	a privileged class of people next in importance to the king
orator	a powerful public speaker
Parlement	a supreme law court of the Ancien Regime
Patriot	someone who wanted the Ancien Regime to be reformed
privilege	rights, benefits or favours belonging to a person or group of people
radical	involving complete and startling change
republic	a country that elects its government and does not have a monach
republican	a person or country in favour of a republic
servitude	slavery
sou	a coin worth five centimes ($1/20$ of a livre)
tyranny	cruel and often unlawful use of power and authority
veteran	someone who has fought in a war

Index